PILOT LADDER MANUAL

BASIC EDITION

WITHERBYS

Since 1740

First edition published 2017

ISBN: 978-1-85609-745-1

© Witherby Publishing Group Ltd, 2017

British Library Cataloguing in Publication Data
A catalogue record for this book is available from the British Library.

Published by

Witherby Publishing Group Ltd
4 Dunlop Square
Livingston, EH54 8SB
Scotland, UK

+44 (0)1506 463 227
info@witherbys.com
witherbys.com

Printed and bound in Great Britain by Martins The Printers, Berwick-upon-Tweed

Contents

Meanings of Symbols used in this Manual

Information on risk assessment topics that can help you plan a safe operation.

Technical information on how to carry out the job correctly.

Important safety observation or comment.

1. Introduction

Throughout the world, at any time of day or night, in good or adverse weather conditions, a number of marine pilots will be in transit either to or from vessels that they have been engaged to safely navigate from one location to another.

The services of a pilot may be required for many reasons, eg providing specialist local navigational knowledge, carrying out ship handling or assisting bridge watchkeepers in high density traffic areas.

Each of these pilots will need to be safely embarked or disembarked from their vessel. There are several ways in which this transfer operation can be completed, each involving a certain degree of risk.

It is critical that all involved in pilot transfer are fully aware of the dangers. Only through effective training and education can pilot transfer operations be made safer, irrespective of the transfer method used.

Pilot embarkation and disembarkation normally takes place when the vessel is underway or alongside a berth, but it may also take place when the vessel is at anchor. Possible transfer methods include by pilot boat, helicopter or directly from the shore. Transfer may be facilitated by the vessel's accommodation ladder or vehicle ramp, or possibly by crane basket. However, the usual method is by traditional wooden pilot ladder, and this arrangement is the focus of this publication.

Despite the best efforts of the International Maritime Pilots' Association (IMPA), various regional and national pilot associations, and the International Maritime Organization (IMO), there continue to be far too many reports of poorly rigged or unsafe pilot ladders.

In recent years, a significant number of pilots have been fatally injured as a direct result of accidents occurring during embarkation or disembarkation and many more have been seriously injured. The safety aspects of rigging a transfer arrangement apply equally to pilots and to seafarers joining and leaving a ship.

The aim of this publication is to remind all seafarers of the vital importance of adhering to the rules for transfer arrangements and of the need to follow established procedures when preparing for the embarkation and disembarkation of pilots. Particular attention should be paid to correct rigging arrangements as these are critical to operational safety.

1.1   Pilot Transfer Rules and Regulations

Two major international legislative documents set out the rules and regulations governing pilot transfer arrangements:

- SOLAS, Chapter V, Safety of Navigation, Regulation 23. This regulates onboard ship requirements for safe deployment of pilot ladder arrangements and associated equipment

- IMO Assembly Resolution A.1045(27). This deals with technical specifications and general dimension requirements for ships' pilot ladders.

Transfer arrangements are also governed by local and national regulations, which may have compliance requirements beyond those specified in SOLAS. Such information should be provided in advance by the pilot station to the ship. In any case, the general rules for safely rigging a pilot transfer arrangement and for conducting pilot transfer apply no matter where in the world the ship is.

> For freeboards of less than 9 m, an individual pilot ladder can be rigged. If greater than 9 m, a combination ladder arrangement will be required. Pilot hoists are prohibited by SOLAS.

The UK Code of Safe Working Practices for Merchant Seafarers (COSWP) provides guidance on pilot transfer arrangements and reference should be made to:

- Chapter 17 – Work at Height

- Chapter 22 – Boarding Arrangements, and in particular:

  o   22.9 – Access for pilots

  o   22.10 – Safe rigging of pilot ladders.

Your company will also set out its own specific rules and procedures in their onboard Safety Management System (SMS). Compliance with these is likely to be the best route to making sure the job is done safely. While good seamanship may well be a matter of practice and experience, it is essential to carry out a risk assessment for every pilot transfer operation. This will help ensure procedures are followed, avoid complacency and reduce the likelihood of an accident occurring.

1.2 Risk Assessment

> A risk assessment will help ensure that all involved in the operation are aware of the potential hazards and the risk of harm to the crew and the pilot. A risk assessment should be carried out by a competent person before work begins on rigging the transfer arrangement.

As a minimum, the risk assessment should:

- Identify all potential hazards, eg strong winds, rough seas, wet decks

- identify who could be harmed, eg seafarers rigging the arrangement, the pilot on the ladder, crew on the pilot boat

- quantify the risk itself, ie the likelihood and severity of the harm occurring

- identify control measures to reduce the risk, eg safety harnesses for crew rigging outboard of the bulwark.

The type of arrangement and, in particular, the weather and sea state may necessitate re-appraisal of the risks of the operation. All involved should be briefed on the risks and control measures, eg wearing of appropriate PPE.

2. Transfer and Rigging Arrangements

All equipment used in pilot transfer must comply with SOLAS Chapter V, Regulation 23 and should be certified in accordance with IMO or ISO standards. This includes the construction as well as any repairs. If in doubt, check the certificates or markings on the equipment. New equipment may still be defective and any concerns must be raised with a senior officer or the company.

All equipment should be thoroughly inspected and checked by a competent person for any signs of damage or defects before and after every operation, as well as on a periodic basis as specified in the company SMS. A deck officer should verify that the arrangements are safely rigged before the ladder is used.

2.1 Pilot Ladders

It should be possible to rig a pilot ladder on either side of the ship. The pilot should be asked to confirm in advance the best side for boarding to allow sufficient time for rigging and checking of the ladder. The ship may decide to rig two ladders, one on either side in case the situation demands it.

Remember that:

- The pilot ladder must be a single length and not joined together with another length of ladder

- there should be no damage, defects, broken steps or spreaders, loose ropes, loose seizings or any non-approved methods of securing.

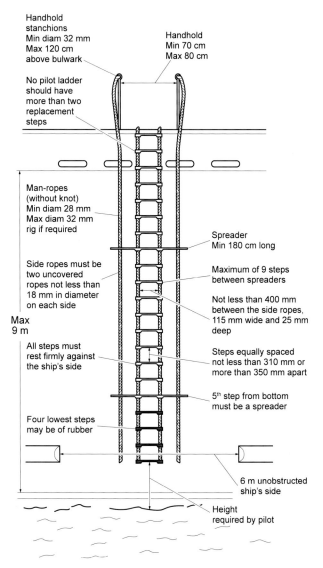

Handhold stanchions
Min diam 32 mm
Max 120 cm above bulwark

Handhold
Min 70 cm
Max 80 cm

No pilot ladder should have more than two replacement steps

Man-ropes (without knot)
Min diam 28 mm
Max diam 32 mm
rig if required

Spreader
Min 180 cm long

Side ropes must be two uncovered ropes not less than 18 mm in diameter on each side

Maximum of 9 steps between spreaders

Not less than 400 mm between the side ropes, 115 mm wide and 25 mm deep

Max 9 m

All steps must rest firmly against the ship's side

Steps equally spaced not less than 310 mm or more than 350 mm apart

5th step from bottom must be a spreader

Four lowest steps may be of rubber

6 m unobstructed ship's side

Height required by pilot

Figure 2.1 - Rigging for freeboards of 9 m or less

2.1.1 General Procedure for Rigging a Pilot Ladder

- Ensure that a risk assessment has been carried out

- ensure that all personnel have adequate PPE

- confirm the side for the ladder and the height required for it to be rigged above the waterline

- if portable, position the ladder on the required side

- remember that, if the freeboard is more than 9 m, the ladder will need to be rigged in a combination arrangement

- check the pilot ladder and its associated equipment for any visible signs of damage or any defects

- if damaged, either replace the ladder entirely or carry out only essential repairs (no more than two replacement steps are permitted) until the ladder can be replaced

- lower the ladder to the required height above the water

- ensure the ladder rests horizontally and against the ship's side

- secure the ladder to the ship using the certified strong points

- if the vessel has a mechanical winch reel, remember to use its supplied securing means to prevent accidental release

- ensure that handhold stanchions, platforms and bulwark ladders are firmly secured to the deck via certified strong points

- deploy man-ropes (without knots) if required by the pilot. Man ropes must be secured to certified strong points

- ensure that the entire arrangement is supervised and inspected by a deck officer prior to boarding of the pilot.

One of the main causes of pilot transfer accidents is improper securing of the pilot ladder.

Always ensure that the ladder is secured firmly to the securing strong point or pad eye on the deck of the ship (and never to the rails or stanchions).

2.1.2   Additional Guidance for Rigging the Ladder

- Ensure that proper and effective maintenance has been carried out regularly on the ladder and its associated equipment. A record should be kept of when the ladder was received, when it was put into service and when inspections, repairs and replacements occur. A sign or notice can show this

Figure 2.2 - Pilot ladder service marking

- consider the number of persons required to carry out the operation safely; always have at least two persons in the job-team to watch over each other

- assess whether the pilot can get from the top of the ladder safely onto the main deck; a properly secured platform or bulwark ladder may be required

- ideally, the ladder should be positioned within the midship half length of the ship

- no shackles, knots or splices are permitted on the side ropes

- the steps must be equally spaced

- the steps must be horizontal

- ensure that the ladder is rigged away from the ship's discharge points, thrusters and propulsion movements

- any chocks or widgets used must be tightly secured

- spreaders must not be lashed between the steps

- side ropes must be equally spaced

- ensure all ropes are tight and secure; loose ropes or loops present a tripping hazard and are not permitted

- ensure steps and spreaders are clean and free from paint and grease so they are not slippery.

2.1.3 Unsafe Pilot Ladders

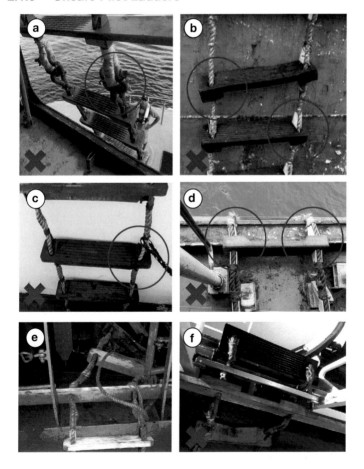

Examples of non-compliant and poorly rigged ladders:

a) two ladders joined by a shackle

b) incorrect repair and rope length

c) broken steps

d) rope seizings chafed and frayed

e) weight of the ladder held by the spreader and not secured

f) ladder held in place by a guillotine bar.

2.2 Combinations and Accommodation Ladders

If the freeboard is greater than 9 m and no side door is available, a combination arrangement will need to be rigged. This involves correctly rigging a pilot ladder in conjunction with the ship's accommodation ladder.

Rigging a combination ladder poses additional risks from working at the ship's side and outboard. Safety harnesses and lifejackets should be worn when rigging the guard ropes on the accommodation ladder, when securing to the ship's side and when attaching hull magnets.

Just as with pilot ladders, accommodation ladders may be dangerous if rigged incorrectly or not maintained. The same general procedure applies as for rigging a pilot ladder, but with the following additional considerations:

- Ensure that personnel are clear of the accommodation ladder and its machinery when it is being lowered/raised

- ensure that the accommodation ladder does not exceed an angle of slope of 45 degrees

- the lower platform of the accommodation ladder must be horizontal and at least 5 m above the sea

- ensure that there is at least 2 m of pilot ladder above the lower platform of the accommodation ladder

- secure the accommodation ladder so it is held firmly to the ship's side by the approved securing method (eg rope lashings to securing points or with hull magnets)

- rig stanchions and guard ropes

- trapdoors if used should be flat and secured.

To assist rigging of a combination ladder, the ship should have a 4 m long visual indicator painted on the side to show the freeboard mark (see Figure 2.3). The use of a heaving line (provided its length is known and measured in metres) can also help with verifying the height above water.

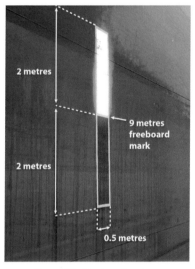

Figure 2.3 - Freeboard mark

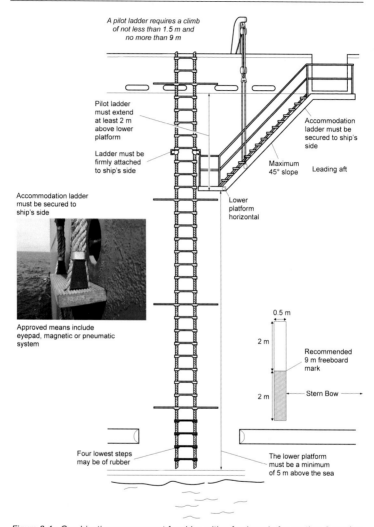

A pilot ladder requires a climb of not less than 1.5 m and no more than 9 m

Pilot ladder must extend at least 2 m above lower platform

Ladder must be firmly attached to ship's side

Accommodation ladder must be secured to ship's side

Accommodation ladder must be secured to ship's side

Maximum 45° slope

Leading aft

Lower platform horizontal

Approved means include eyepad, magnetic or pneumatic system

0.5 m

2 m

Recommended 9 m freeboard mark

2 m

Stern Bow

Four lowest steps may be of rubber

The lower platform must be a minimum of 5 m above the sea

Figure 2.4 - Combination arrangement for ships with a freeboard of more than 9 m when no side door is available

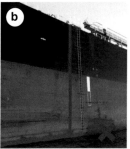

Examples of non-compliant and poorly rigged combination ladders:

a) the accommodation ladder is less than 5 m from the waterline, causing problems for safe clearance of the pilot boat

b) failure to rig a combination ladder when the ship has a large freeboard (this example would involve a climb of 17 m!)

c) the lower platform is not horizontal.

2.3 Shipside Doors

Large ships with high freeboards are often fitted with shipside doors to enable the pilot to transfer directly into the ship. These doors eliminate the need to rig a combination arrangement and reduce the vertical climb for pilots.

The procedure for safe rigging of a pilot ladder is still required, even when used with a shipside door. In addition:

- Ship doors used for pilot transfer should not open outwards

- the access position and adjacent area should be clear of obstructions, including the pilot ladder winch reel

- ensure that personnel are clear when opening and closing the door and using any machinery

- during pilot transfer, the door should be secured to prevent it from closing or swinging

- after operations, the door should be verified as closed and locked so the watertight integrity of the ship is maintained.

Shipside doors should not be used if they do not allow the ladder to be rigged safely. In image a), the ladder is not flush with the ship. In image b), the shipside door is hazardous because it opens outwards.

3. Other Equipment

3.1 Personal Protective Equipment (PPE)

PPE is a requirement for safe operations for anyone using the transfer arrangements and ladders. This includes pilots, any other persons embarking or disembarking and ship's personnel when rigging the transfer arrangements. As a minimum, all personnel should wear the following PPE:

- An inflatable lifejacket, checked operable and fitted with a light; if fitted with a crotch strap, this should be used

- non-slip footwear that will not come loose easily, eg tied with laces

- safety helmets or hard hats, as required

- clothing that will be visible if the wearer falls into the water, eg trimmed with retroreflective strips.

In addition, ships' personnel who are rigging the transfer arrangements, particularly while working outboard to rig a combination ladder, should utilise a properly worn and secured safety harness. A second person should monitor their safety and they should be in communication with the bridge via UHF radio.

Figure 3.1 - Correct use of PPE

> Never take an unnecessary risk by carrying out an operation without the appropriate PPE. Plan ahead for what you need to complete the job safely.

3.2   Man-ropes

Man-ropes (see Figure 3.2) should be kept ready for immediate use if required by the pilot. They are commonly used in areas that experience large swell heights. When using man-ropes, it should be ensured that:

- The man-ropes are not longer than the pilot ladder itself

- they do not trail or hang in the water

- they reach the stanchions or bulwarks at the main point of access

- they are properly secured to certified strong points on the deck

- they have no additional decorations, eg knots, plastic sheathing or canvas

- they are no loose ropes or loops that may present a tripping hazard

- if a temporary platform is used to cover any rope excess on deck, it is properly secured.

Figure 3.2 - Man-ropes

3.3   Lifebuoys and Self-igniting Lights

A lifebuoy with a line and a self-igniting light should be positioned close to the pilot transfer position, so that it is immediately accessible if a person falls into the water during the rigging or the transfer process.

The lifebuoy and light may be part of the ship's life saving appliance (LSA) arrangements or may be additional.

Figure 3.3 - Lifebuoy positioned close to the pilot transfer position

A lifebuoy line should never be made fast to the ship; it is unlikely that a casualty will swim at the same speed as the ship. It should be kept free to be quickly thrown in the event of an emergency.

3.4   Lighting, Heaving Lines and Retrieval Lines

3.4.1   Lighting

Adequate lighting must be provided to illuminate the transfer arrangements over side and the position on deck where a person embarks or disembarks. This may include:

- Fitted lights, such as outward swinging searchlights on the bridge wing or at the pilot ladder itself

- portable torches for use during the transfer process.

3.4.2   Heaving Lines

Many pilots when embarking or disembarking will require the use of a
heaving line to transfer either personal effects or navigation equipment.
A heaving line should be kept close at hand in case needed.

3.4.3   Retrieval Lines

Retrieval lines are sometimes used to help recover long pilot ladders after
use. If not properly tended, retrieval lines (sometimes called tripping lines)
may present a tripping hazard for the pilot boarding and the launch crew and
may also foul the pilot launch. Lines should be from forward.

Retrieval lines must always be rigged clear of the pilot transfer
operational area and must not be attached to the bottom of the
pilot ladder.

If a retrieval line is improperly secured leading aft, there is a risk
of it being trapped or caught between the pilot launch and the
vessel's hull, potentially pulling the ladder backwards during the
transfer.

*Figure 3.4 - a) Incorrect fixing of a retrieval line to the pilot ladder (also note that the pilot
in image a) is not wearing a lifejacket or other flotation aid)
b) incorrect fixing of a retrieval line to the bottom of the ladder*

4. Safe Operations

4.1 Consequences of Incorrect Rigging

Challenges and consequences of incorrectly rigged ladders

Embarking and disembarking from a ship via a pilot ladder is a complex manoeuvre that requires good balance and coordination.

Challenges

Climbing a considerable height using a free-hanging pilot ladder provided by a high-sided vessel that is underway can be a physically challenging operation with the following potential complications:

- When climbing a ladder for embarkation onto a vessel, the first opportunity for the pilot to view the securing arrangement is when they reach the deck. Prior to that, they rely on blind trust of the ship's crew

- after the potentially tiring physical climb, it is necessary to reach and transfer off the ladder onto the

Consequences

- A pilot or other person may be seriously injured

- a pilot may decline to board a ship that presents an incorrectly rigged, defective or poorly positioned ladder. This will cause a loss of time for the ship and result in financial losses for the shipowner

- defects or deficiencies must be reported by the pilot to port State authorities, which could lead to a full Port State Control inspection. This will also cause a time delay for the ship and may result in financial penalties for the shipowner.

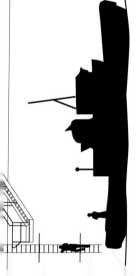

- the ladder may be moving in different planes, vertically, laterally and trying to twist

- if the ladder is rigged correctly, it will be hanging vertically alongside the vessel, but it is still flexible and not rigid

- the pilot boat and the ship may be moving at different speeds and with different independent rolling and pitching motions

- although it may be easier to climb down a ladder, it is often more hazardous because it can be more difficult to judge the right time to step across to the pilot boat.

Transfer operations can be significantly more hazardous:

During hours of darkness

in a rough seaway with large waves and swell

in adverse weather conditions

in low air and seawater temperatures.

4.2 Guidance on Maintenance and Storage

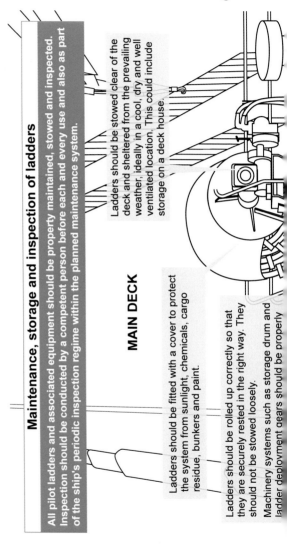

Maintenance, storage and inspection of ladders

All pilot ladders and associated equipment should be properly maintained, stowed and inspected. Inspection should be conducted by a competent person before each and every use and also as part of the ship's periodic inspection regime within the planned maintenance system.

Ladders should be stowed clear of the deck and sheltered from the prevailing weather, ideally in a cool, dry and well ventilated location. This could include storage on a deck house.

MAIN DECK

Ladders should be fitted with a cover to protect the system from sunlight, chemicals, cargo residue, bunkers and paint.

Ladders should be rolled up correctly so that they are securely rested in the right way. They should not be stowed loosely.

Machinery systems such as storage drum and ladder deployment gears should be properly

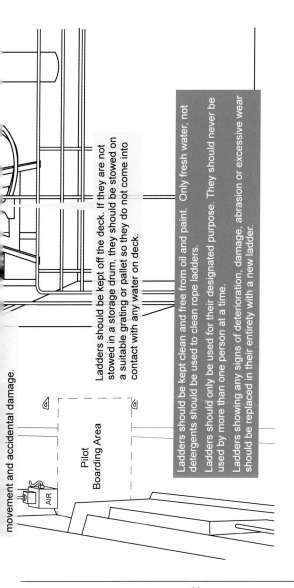

movement and accidental damage.

Ladders should be kept off the deck. If they are not stowed in a storage drum, they should be stowed on a suitable grating or pallet so they do not come into contact with any water on deck.

Ladders should be kept clean and free from oil and paint. Only fresh water, not detergents should be used to clean rope ladders.

Ladders should only be used for their designated purpose. They should never be used by more than one person at a time.

Ladders showing any signs of deterioration, damage, abrasion or excessive wear should be replaced in their entirety with a new ladder.

Pilot
Boarding Area

AIR

4.3   Supervision and the Transfer Process

The rigging of the pilot transfer arrangements and the embarkation of a pilot must be supervised by a responsible officer having means of communication with the navigation bridge. This officer must also arrange for the escort of the pilot by a safe route to and from the navigation bridge.

Personnel engaged in rigging and operating any mechanical equipment should be instructed in the safe procedures to be adopted. The equipment should be tested before use.

4.3.1   The Deck Party

On some cargo vessels, it is common to find that a cadet is used to stand in for a responsible officer, and passenger vessels often use a security officer in a similar manner. Although cadets and security officers may be suitable for escort duties between the bridge and the pilot access position, they are not considered to be responsible officers for supervision purposes. The inspection of the arrangements and the boarding of the pilot must be supervised by an STCW certificated officer.

The supervising officer should not be the sole member of the deck party. If a last-minute change needs to be made to the ladder position or height or to transfer a pilot's personal effects, it is essential that an additional crew member is available to provide assistance.

A deck party should, at a minimum, consist of a supervising officer and at least one other crew member. Ideally, two crew members should rig the ladder and an officer should separately supervise and inspect the arrangement after the rigging and should then monitor the pilot boarding.

4.3.2   Communications

The responsible officer supervising the transfer should be in direct contact with the bridge. If this contact is by radio, it is important that radio working channels are established. All radios (and their batteries) must be checked before use.

Clear and concise communication between the supervising officer and the navigation bridge is of particular importance on large vessels or where clear line of sight is not possible. Remote CCTV cameras can be used beneficially if fitted.

When boarding a pilot from a boat, it is good practice for the supervising officer to advise the navigation bridge of:

- The approach of the pilot boat

- when the pilot is on the ladder

- when the pilot is safely on board

- when the pilot boat is clear.

When a pilot is disembarking by boat, the officer should advise:

- When the pilot boat is alongside

- when the pilot is on the ladder

- when the pilot is on the pilot boat

- when the pilot boat is clear.

Before transferring from the pilot boat to the vessel, it is important for the pilot to ascertain from the supervising officer that the ladder is properly secured.

4.3.3　Checks After Rigging

The officer should make a thorough check of the entire boarding arrangements before allowing the pilot to board. He should ask the question "Would I climb it myself?". The officer should confirm that the ladder is correctly rigged to the pilot boat before allowing the pilot to board. See Section 5 - Checklists for details of the checks that should be completed before, during and after every pilot transfer.

4.4　Safe Deck Access

Access between the pilot ladder and the ship's deck is the key aspect of the pilot transfer arrangement.

The ship must provide safe, convenient and unobstructed passage between the head of the ladder and the ship's deck.

If access is via a gateway in the rails or bulwark, adequate handholds must be provided.

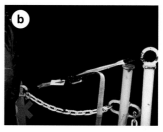

Figure 4.1 - a) Correct and b) incorrect presentation of gateway

If a gateway cannot be provided, the ship is required to provide a bulwark ladder with two handhold stanchions rigidly secured to the ship's structure at or near their bases and at higher points. The bulwark ladder should be securely attached to the ship to prevent overturning.

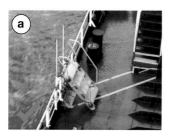

Figure 4.2 - a) Correctly fitted bulwark ladder
b) The pilot should never have to jump!

Head the vessel in a direction and speed as instructed by the pilot authority, but at all times be aware of and monitor the movements of other vessels in the area.

Maintain continuous communication between the supervising deck officer and the navigation bridge.

Rig the pilot ladder at a height above the water directed by the pilot boat. Always rig the pilot ladder in strict accordance with SOLAS V 23. All crew involved in rigging of the ladder arrangement must be trained to recognise and understand the risks involved and the requirements of the legislation.

Ensure that supervision of embarkation and disembarkation is always undertaken by a responsible deck officer, positioned at the point of access.

The pilot access point should be unobstructed and free from loose objects or other hazards.

Rig the pilot ladder on the side of the vessel directed by the pilot boat, to give the best lee side.

Ensure that all equipment is inspected prior to rigging and that the deployment is supervised by a responsible deck officer.

Ensure safe, appropriate and unobstructed passage for the pilot from the embarkation point to and from the bridge (as outlined in red).

The engine room should be in a manned condition with engines on standby. The communication protocol between the bridge and the engine room must be established.

5. Checklists

5.1 Rigging a Safe Transfer Arrangement	Tick
Has a risk assessment been carried out prior to the operation for all aspects of the job? (*See Section 1.2 for further guidance.*)	
Has the pilot station been contacted to determine boarding location, ship side and height of the ladder above the water?	
Is the vessel freeboard greater than 9 m? If so, a combination arrangement will be required.	
Is the equipment SOLAS approved and maintained regularly and correctly as part of the ship's planned maintenance?	
Are all personnel briefed and instructed on how to use the equipment and carry out the job safely?	
Do all personnel have adequate PPE, including safety harnesses and lifejackets as required?	
Has all the equipment been thoroughly inspected and checked by an officer to confirm that it is in good condition? *Any damage or defects should be rectified and if necessary the ladder replaced entirely.*	
When the ladder has been lowered, has it been confirmed that it is at the right height above the water and resting horizontally and flat against the ship's side?	
Has the ladder been properly secured by an approved method? *This should involve ropes or shackles to the strong point of the ship. Non-approved methods should not be used. (See Section 2.1 for further guidance.)*	
Has the winch, reel or any mechanical systems used to be secured to prevent accidental operation or release?	
Are there adequate handhold stanchions or a properly secured bulwark ladder for access to the deck?	
If a platform is fitted, is it horizontal and properly secured?	
Are any retrieval lines attached to only the lower spreader, leading forward and well clear of the pilot boat area?	
Is the route to the bridge clear of dangers and obstructions?	
Are man-ropes deployed if required?	
Has the officer confirmed that all arrangements are safely rigged, adequate and in compliance with the rules and regulations?	

5.2 Transferring a Pilot to and from the Ship | Tick

Is a certified officer supervising the operation?	
Are there adequate communications in place between the bridge, pilot boarding area and pilot boat? *The officer should have radio contact and the equipment should be tested before use.*	
Is there adequate illumination covering the ladder arrangement, boarding area and route to the bridge?	
Is a life-buoy and heaving line situated close by, ready for use if required?	

The officer should confirm to the pilot boat/pilot that it is safe to use the ladder and inform the bridge of each stage of the operation. (See Section 4.3.2 for further guidance.) The pilot should be escorted at all times, whether embarking or disembarking.

5.3 Post Operations | Tick

Do all personnel still have adequate PPE and are they all still briefed and instructed about how to do the job safely?	
Has the ladder been recovered and rolled up correctly?	
Has the equipment been inspected by a competent person after use? *This should include a thorough visual examination of the ladder and all arrangements, as damage may have occurred during the transfer operation.*	
Has the ladder been stored away from the ship's side and suitably protected from the weather?	
Have the ladder and other arrangements been stowed away and secured to prevent damage while at sea?	
Have any repairs been carried out if required? *Repairs should not exceed the requirements in SOLAS V 23.*	